What in the World Is a Clarinet?

Mary Elizabeth Salzmann

Consulting Editor, Diane Craig, M.A./Reading Specialist

A Division of ABDO

ABDO
Publishing Company

visit us at www.abdopublishing.com

Published by ABDO Publishing Company, a division of ABDO, P.O. Box 398166, Minneapolis, Minnesota 55439. Copyright © 2012 by Abdo Consulting Group, Inc. International copyrights reserved in all countries. No part of this book may be reproduced in any form without written permission from the publisher. Super SandCastle™ is a trademark and logo of ABDO Publishing Company.

Printed in the United States of America, North Mankato, Minnesota
092011
012012

 PRINTED ON RECYCLED PAPER

Editor: Elissa Mann
Content Developer: Nancy Tuminelly
Cover and Interior Design and Production: Colleen Dolphin, Mighty Media, Inc.
Photo Credits: Colleen Dolphin, iStockphoto (Byron Carlson, ene, Thomas Shortell), Shutterstock, Thinkstock

Library of Congress Cataloging-in-Publication Data

Salzmann, Mary Elizabeth, 1968-

  What in the world is a clarinet? / Mary Elizabeth Salzmann.

    p. cm. -- (Musical instruments)

  ISBN 978-1-61783-203-1

  1. Clarinet--Juvenile literature. I. Title.

  ML945.S25 2012

  788.6'219--dc23

                    2011023167

Super SandCastle™ books are created by a team of professional educators, reading specialists, and content developers around five essential components— phonemic awareness, phonics, vocabulary, text comprehension, and fluency—to assist young readers as they develop reading skills and strategies and increase their general knowledge. All books are written, reviewed, and leveled for guided reading, early reading intervention, and Accelerated Reader® programs for use in shared, guided, and independent reading and writing activities to support a balanced approach to literacy instruction.

Contents

What Is a

A clarinet is a
musical instrument.

Clarinet?

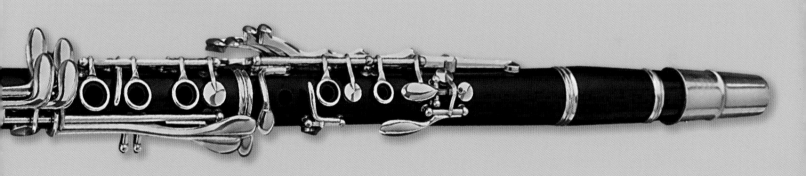

A clarinet can be separated into five pieces. They are the mouthpiece, the barrel, the upper **joint**, the lower joint, and the bell.

mouthpiece

barrel

bell

upper joint

lower joint

A clarinet has a reed.

The reed goes on the mouthpiece.

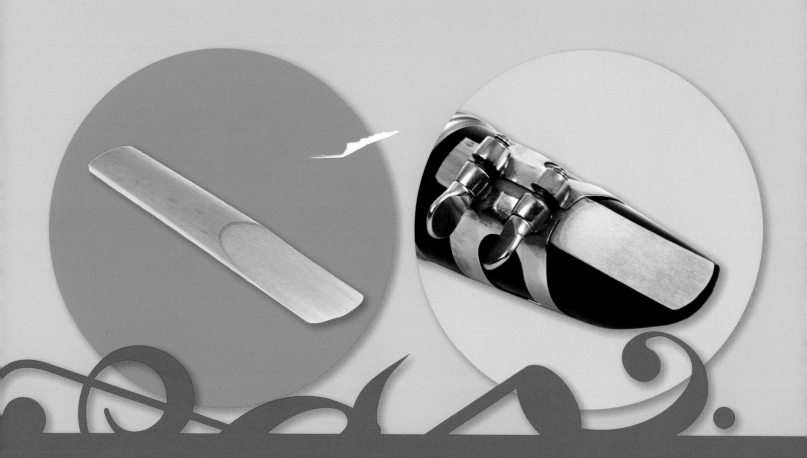

The reed has to be wet before it is used. The clarinet player holds it in his or her mouth for a few seconds.

Then the clarinet player **attaches** the reed to the mouthpiece.

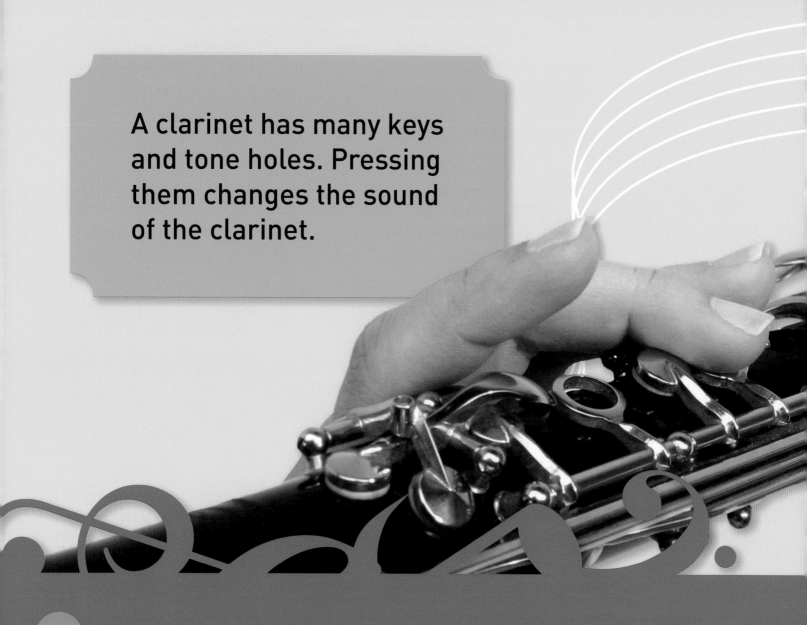

A clarinet has many keys and tone holes. Pressing them changes the sound of the clarinet.

To play the clarinet, the clarinet player blows into the mouthpiece. He or she presses the keys and tone holes to play different notes.

Let's Play

14

the Clarinet!

Carter is practicing a song on the clarinet. He is playing in a school concert on Wednesday.

Diego plays the clarinet in the marching band. He can march and play at the same time!

Molly is at her clarinet **lesson**. Her teacher helps her read the **sheet music**. The sheet music says which notes to play.

Nicole is done playing her clarinet. Now she will take it **apart** and put it away. Each piece fits into a space in the clarinet case.

Find the Clarinet

a.

b.

c.

d.

Clarinet Quiz

1. Clarinets have five pieces. True or False?

2. A clarinet has a reed. True or False?

3. A clarinet player blows into the mouthpiece to play it. True or False?

4. Carter's school concert is on Tuesday. True or False?

5. Molly does not read **sheet music** at her **lesson**. True or False?

Glossary

apart – in or into two or more pieces.

attach – to join or connect.

joint – a part with one or more ends that can be connected to another part.

lesson – a period of time when a skill or topic is studied or taught.

sheet music – a sheet of paper with the notes to a song printed on it.